QUEEN ELIZABETH'S GRAMMAR SCHOOL
FAVERSHAM

Date	Form	Name

All books lost or damaged must be replaced

2805/BH

JOSEPH HAYDN
Eleven Late String Quartets
Opp. 74, 76 and 77, Complete

JOSEPH HAYDN

Eleven Late String Quartets

Opp. 74, 76 and 77, Complete

Edited by Wilhelm Altmann

Dover Publications, Inc.

New York

This Dover edition, first published in 1979, is an unabridged republication of eleven separate quartet volumes (Op. 74, Nos. 1-3; Op. 76, Nos. 1-6; and Op. 77, Nos. 1 & 2) as published by Ernst Eulenburg Ltd., London (n.d.; publication numbers 146, 147, 58, 69, 10, 3, 56, 57, 191, 61 and 355, respectively, of the Edition Eulenburg, or Eulenburg Miniature Scores).

International Standard Book Number: 0-486-23753-2
Library of Congress Catalog Card Number: 78-67400

Manufactured in the United States of America
Dover Publications, Inc.
180 Varick Street
New York, N.Y. 10014

Contents

Opus 74

("Apponyi Quartets," dedicated to Count Apponyi, composed 1793)

No. 1,   in C Major
 Allegro moderato   page 1
 Andantino grazioso   10
 Menuetto. Allegretto   16
 Finale. Vivace   19

No. 2,   in F Major
 Allegro spirituoso   29
 Andante grazioso   40
 Menuetto. Allegretto   46
 Finale. Presto   49

No. 3,   in G Minor ("Horseman")
 Allegro   59
 Largo assai   68
 Menuetto. Allegretto   71
 Finale. Allegro con brio   74

Opus 76

("Erdődy Quartets," dedicated to Count Erdődy, composed 1796/7)

No. 1,   in G Major
 Allegro con spirito   83
 Adagio sostenuto   93
 Menuetto. Presto   100
 Allegro ma non troppo   102

No. 2,   in D Minor ("Quinten")
 Allegro   113
 Andante o più tosto allegretto   122
 Menuetto. Allegro ma non troppo   128
 Vivace assai   131

No. 3,   in C Major ("Emperor")
 Allegro   139
 Poco adagio; cantabile   150
 Menuetto. Allegro   156
 Finale. Presto   159

No. 4,   in B-flat Major ("Sunrise")
 Allegro con spirito   169
 Adagio   180
 Menuetto. Allegro   184
 Finale. Allegro, ma non troppo   188

No. 5, in D Major
    Allegretto   page 197
    Largo. Cantabile e mesto   205
    Menuetto. Allegro   210
    Finale. Presto   212

No. 6, in E-flat Major
    Allegretto — Allegro   221
    Fantasia. Adagio   229
    Menuetto. Presto   233
    Finale. Allegro spirituoso   238

Opus 77

("Lobkowitz Quartets," dedicated to Prince von Lobkowitz, composed 1799)

No. 1, in G Major
    Allegro moderato   245
    Adagio   255
    Menuetto. Presto   260
    Finale. Presto   266

No. 2, in F Major
    Allegro moderato   275
    Menuetto. Presto, ma non troppo   286
    Andante   290
    Finale. Vivace assai   297

Op. 74, No. 1, in C Major

I

Op. 74, No. 1   3

Op. 74, No. 1   7

II

Andantino grazioso

III

Menuetto D.C.
al Fine.

IV

Finale
Vivace

Op. 74, No. 2, in F Major

I.

Op. 74, No. 2   31

II.

Andante grazioso. ♩ = 92.

III.

Finale.
Presto. ♩= 48.

IV.

Op. 74, No. 3, in G Minor ("Horseman")

I

II

Largo assai

III

Menuetto. Allegretto

Menuetto D.C. al 𝄐

IV

Finale. Allegro con brio

Op. 76, No. 1, in G Major

I

Allegro con spirito

II

Adagio sostenuto

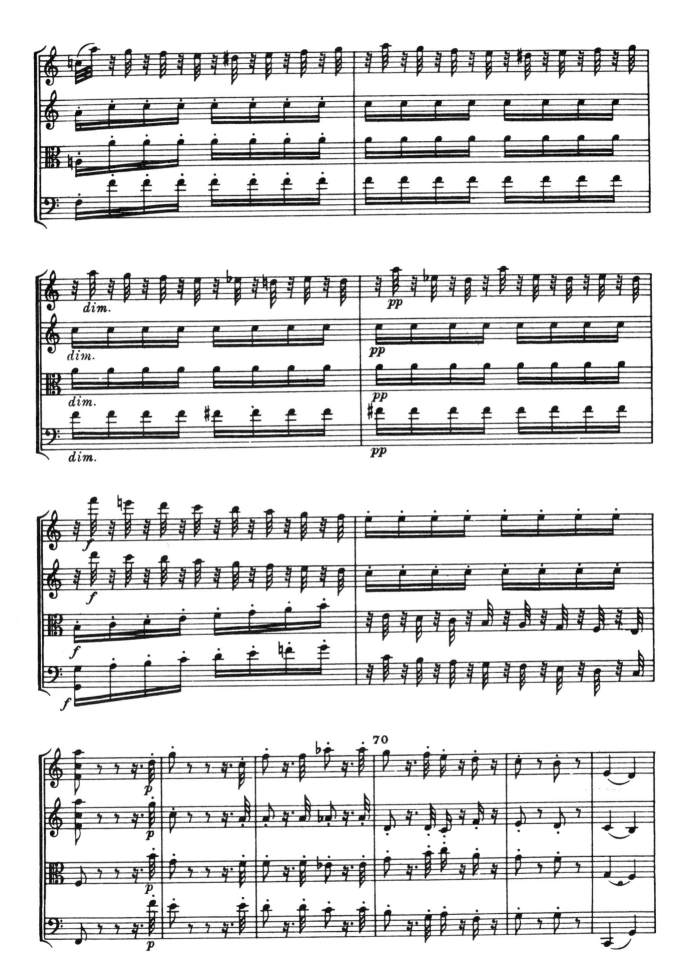

III

Menuetto
Presto

IV

Allegro ma non troppo

Op. 76, No. 2, in D Minor ("Quinten")

I

II

Andante o più tosto allegretto

60

III

Menuetto. Allegro ma non troppo.

IV

Vivace assai.

Op. 76, No. 3, in C Major ("Emperor")

I

144   Op. 76, No. 3

la seconda volta più presto

Var. II

Var. III

III

Menuett. Allegro

IV

Finale. Presto

Op. 76, No. 4, in B-flat Major ("Sunrise")

I

Allegro con spirito

Op. 76, No. 4   175

II

Adagio

III

Menuetto. Allegro

M. D. C.

IV

Finale. Allegro, ma non troppo

Op. 76, No. 4   195

Op. 76, No. 5, in D Major

I

II

Largo. Cantabile e mesto

III

Menuetto. Allegro

Trio

Menuetto D.C.

IV

Finale. Presto

Op. 76, No. 6, in E-flat Major

I

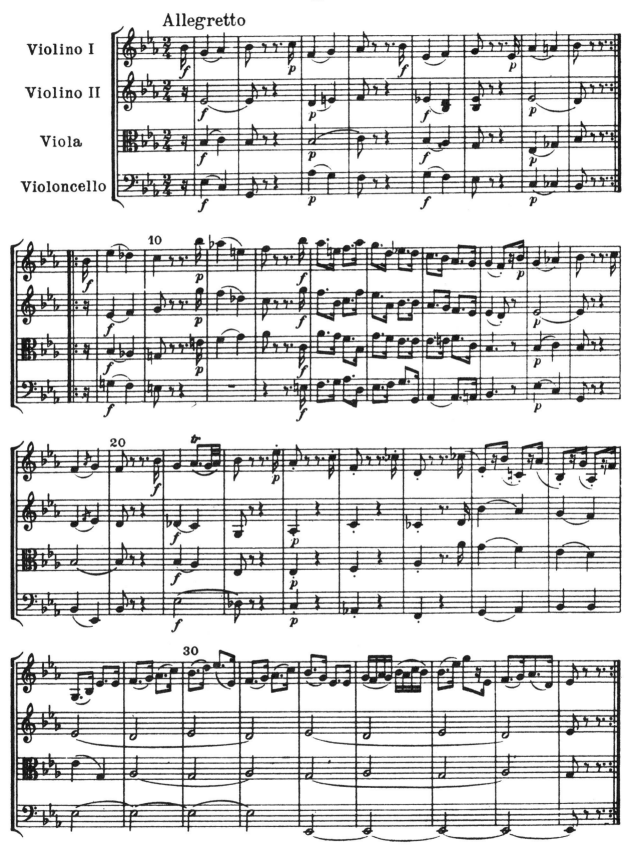

Fantasia
Adagio

III

Menuetto
Presto

IV

Finale
Allegro spirituoso

Op. 77, No. 1, in G Major

I

Allegro moderato

II

Adagio

Menuetto
Presto

Menuetto D.C. al Fine

IV

Finale
Presto

Op. 77, No. 2, in F Major

I

II

Menuetto. Presto, ma non troppo

Coda

III

120

IV

Finale. Vivace assai

10